Parents

IRRESPONSIBLE

Insects and Spiders

Alix Wood

Gareth Stevens PUBLISHING

Please visit our website, www.garethstevens.com. For a free color catalog of all our high-quality books, call toll free 1-800-542-2595 or fax 1-877-542-2596.

Cataloging-in-Publication Data
Names: Wood, Alix.
Title: Irresponsible insects and spiders / Alix Wood.
Description: Buffalo, NY : Gareth Stevens Publishing, 2027. |
Series: Nature's worst parents | Includes glossary and index.
Identifiers: ISBN 9781482477658 (pbk.) | ISBN 9781482477665 (library bound) |
ISBN 9781482477672 (ebook)
Subjects: LCSH: Insects--Juvenile literature. | Spiders--Juvenile literature.
Classification: LCC QL467.2 W65 2027 | DDC 595.7--dc23

Published in 2027 by
Gareth Stevens Publishing
2544 Clinton St.
Buffalo, NY 14224

Designed and written by Alix Wood

Picture Credits: all illustrations © Alix Wood;

Photo credits — cover except bottom right, 5, 6 main, 8, 10, 18, 23, 28 top © Adobe Stock Images; cover bottom right © Gail Hampshire/Creative Commons; 4 © Shutterstock; 6 top © Oliver Koemmerling/Creative Commons; 9 top © Calle Eklund/Creative Commons; 12 top © PJC and Co/Creative Commons; 12 bottom © Tartally A, Koschuh A, Varga Z//Creative Commons; 14, 21, 31 © www.naturepl.com; 17 © Olaf Leillinger/Creative Commons; 18 © photochem PA/Creative Commons; 20 © Aj Cann/Creative Commons; 22 © Greg Hume/Creative Commons; 24 © Duwwel/ Creative Commons; 25, 29 © Charles J. Sharp/Creative Commons; 26 © Peter Riujs Fotografie/Creative Commons; 28 bottom © Jesse Rorabaugh; 30 top © H005/Creative Commons; 30 bottom © Adrian Tync/Creative Commons

Printed in China
CPSIA compliance information: Batch #QS27GS: For further information contact Gareth Stevens at 1-800-542-2595.

Find us on

Contents

WHAT ARE INSECTS?

Dragonflies, beetles, bees, and ants are all insects. Insects have six legs. They have feelers, called **antennae**, that help them find their way around.

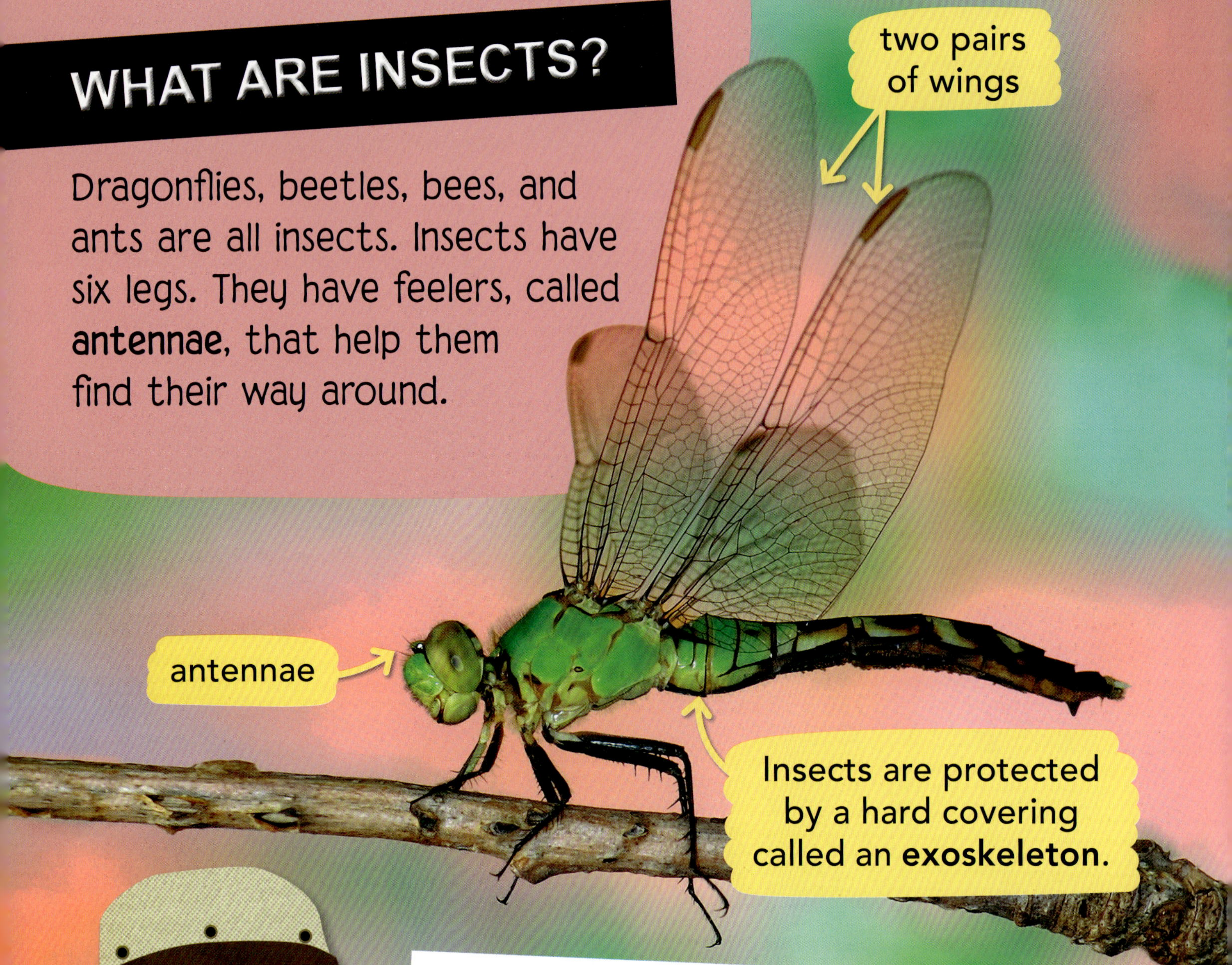

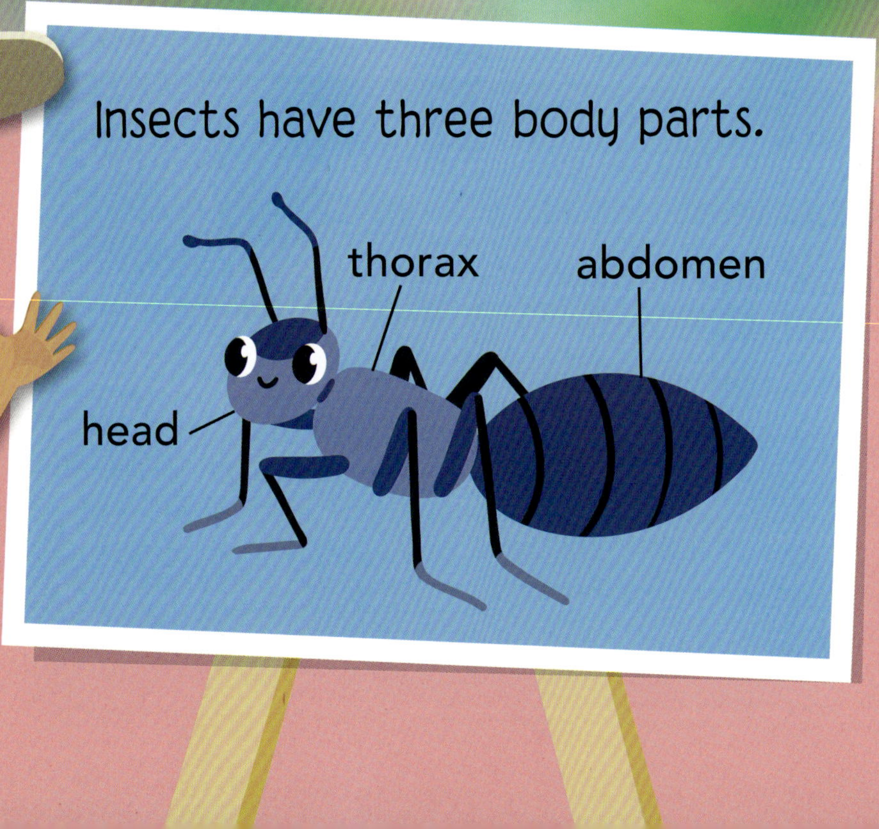

Most insect babies develop in four stages.

The insect mom lays her eggs.

The eggs hatch into wiggly, hungry **larvae**.

Each larva builds a pupa. Inside it, they change into an adult.

The adult insect emerges from the **pupa**.

WHAT ARE SPIDERS?

A spider mom carries her babies on her back.

Spiders eat insects! Spiders have eight thin legs. Their body has just two parts, rather than three.

Most spiders spin webs to trap insects. They kill their prey with **venom** or wrap it alive to keep it from escaping.

Insects and spiders CAN be great parents, but they also do some pretty irresponsible things!

Praying Mantis

Praying mantis parents don't really get along. Once a praying mantis mom has found the perfect dad for her babies, he better watch out!

The females are much larger than the males.

Female praying mantises usually eat their mate. They often bite his head right off!

Why Do They Do That?

The mom eats the dad to make sure she has enough energy to lay her eggs. While this isn't the best news for dad, at least he gave his kids the best start in life!

The mom lays her eggs in a frothy liquid that dries into a hard case. The mom then dies over winter. The eggs will hatch in the spring.

Even if the parents survived winter, they wouldn't care for their babies. They are more likely to eat them!

WHAT?

Praying mantis babies may eat each other, too, if there is not much food around when they hatch!

Burying Beetles

These colorful beetles get their name because they like burying things! They are also sometimes called sexton beetles.

The mom and dad beetles use their antennae to sniff out small dead animals. Then, they bury them!

I RAISE MY KIDS IN A DEAD MOUSE!

WHAT?

Why do they bury dead animals? Because mom wants to lay her eggs in the rotting carcass. Lovely!

Why Do They Do That?

The dead animal makes a great meal for the larvae when they hatch. Mom and dad eat some of the carcass and then throw it up. The lucky little larvae get to eat the vomit!

Sadly, there may not be enough vomit for everyone. Larvae that bother mom and dad the most get fed.

But watch out! Mom and dad may eat a larva if it annoys them too much. They will eat all the unfed larvae too.

Froghoppers

Froghopper moms lay their eggs on plants their larvae will like to eat. So far, so good. Then, they just leave them there!

Froghoppers may not be great moms, but they have an amazing skill. The tiny bugs can leap 27.5 inches (70 cm) into the air! That's like a person jumping over a skyscraper!

MY LARVAE MAKE THIS SPIT-LIKE FOAM TO HIDE IN!

You can see why froghoppers are also called spittlebugs!

WHAT?

The foam isn't actually spit. It comes from a larva's other end! The larva forces air into each juicy mouthful of plant matter. Then, it squeezes juicy bubbles out of its behind!

Why Do They Do That?

Because of where it came from, the froghopper's foam doesn't smell or taste very good! The bitter taste helps protect the larva from any predators.

The larva can hide in the foam and breathe air from the bubbles. The foam helps keep the larva cool in hot weather and warm in cold weather too. So, maybe they don't really need great parents?

Large Blue Butterflies

These rare butterflies lay their eggs on wild thyme plants. Why? Red ants usually live under this tasty herb.

I LET RED ANTS RAISE MY BABIES!

The eggs hatch, and the baby caterpillars eat some thyme. Then, they drop to the ground and release a sweet-smelling scent. The scent tricks red ants into believing the caterpillars are their babies.

wild thyme

The ants carry the caterpillars into their nest.

WHAT?

Once it has tricked its way into the nest, the caterpillar starts eating the ant larvae! It eats the big ones first, giving the small ones time to grow. This way, the food supply lasts longer!

After the caterpillar has eaten around a thousand ant larvae, it makes a pupa, or chrysalis. Inside, it imitates a queen ant's noises, so the ants will keep taking care of it!

As the butterfly starts to emerge, the ants even help it out of the nest.

Why Do They Do That?

Many insects don't stick around to raise their babies. At least this butterfly leaves its eggs where there will be food for them as they hatch and grow!

Dracula Ants

These ants have the fastest jaws of any animal. They kill all kinds of tasty prey. However, the adult ants can't eat the bugs they catch. Their waists are too small for solid food to pass through. Instead, they feed the prey to their larvae.

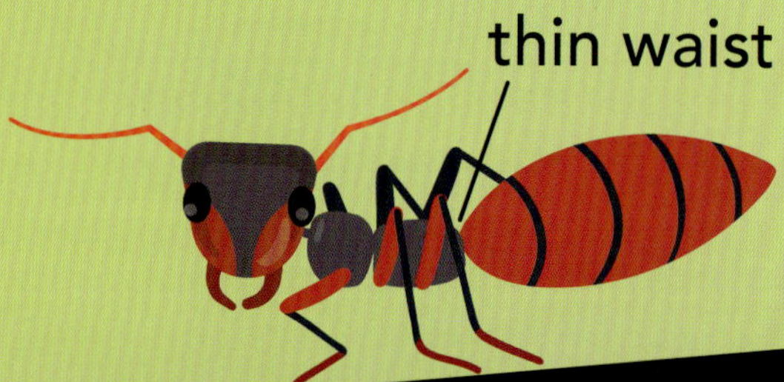

Lucky larvae? Hmm. maybe not. The ants want something in return. Blood!

I BITE MY LARVA AND DRINK ITS BLOOD!

WHAT?

Adult dracula ants bite a hole in their larva's skin with their strong jaws. They suck out its blood and feed it to their ant colony.

The bites don't kill the larvae, but they do leave scars. And the larvae learn there is no such thing as a free lunch.

Why Do They Do That?

In a dracula ant colony, everyone does what they do best. The adults hunt. The queen is busy laying eggs. Larvae act as the colony's food processor. When the adults need a snack, they just bite a larva!

Scientists believe that having less blood may shield the larva from some infections.

Leaf Miners

A lot of insects lay their eggs on leaves. When their larvae hatch, they have a tasty leaf meal waiting for them. The larva can crawl around looking for different types of leaves to eat. But leaf miner larvae do something unusual when they hatch.

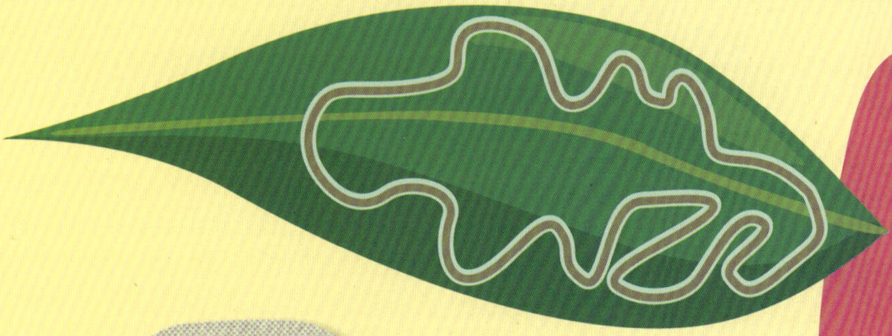

Tiny leaf miner larvae bore into the leaf their eggs were laid on.

Why Do They Do That?

Burrowing into the leaf means the tiny larvae won't get washed away by rain or blown away by wind. The leaf protects them from heat and cold, as well as the sun's harmful rays. But their whole life depends on one single leaf.

WHAT?

Most leaf miner moms lay their eggs on leaves their larvae can eat. But some moms choose diseased plants or leaves the larvae can't eat. The larvae are trapped in their leaf, so a bad leaf choice by mom means they won't survive.

MOM LAID ME ON A USELESS LEAF!

The tiny leafminer moth chooses to lay its eggs on ash, privet, jasmine, or lilac trees. Moms that choose ash leaves may have made a bad choice. Many ash trees have a disease, so the larvae may not get a healthy leaf.

leafminer moth's actual size

Desert Spiders

Desert spiders build cone-shaped webs near plants that attract insects. The insects caught in the web make a tasty snack.

a desert spider mom in her web

a grasshopper caught in a web

The mom makes a silk egg sac and lays her eggs in it. She helps the baby spiders, called spiderlings, when they hatch.

WHAT?

A male spider may eat spiderlings or destroy an egg sac if the spiderlings aren't his.

Mom gets back at dad! Female desert spiders will sometimes eat the much smaller males.

MOM FEEDS US HER VOMIT!

Once the babies hatch, the desert spider mom serves them a pretty gross dinner.

Special chemicals in her body break down the food she ate. The chemicals also break down bits of her own body!

She turns all this into a lovely meal for her babies—yummy spider vomit!

Why Do They Do That?

This vomit meal is very nutritious. The young spiderlings grow to three times their original size after two weeks of eating this "special" snack.

Desert spider moms' insides keep breaking down. **Read what happens to them, and the black lace-weaver spider, on pages 20 and 21.**

Black Lace-Weaver Spiders

Black lace-weaver spiders lay special eggs to feed their young spiderlings. Called **trophic eggs**, this type of egg can't hatch into spiders. Mom just lays them as food for her babies.

Once the spiderlings have eaten all the eggs, they need something else to eat!

black lace-weaver spider mom

The spider mom drums the web with her feet, calling the spiderlings to her.

Mom presses her body onto the spiderlings, encouraging them to feed on her!

WHAT?

The spiderlings start to eat their mom! As they eat, the spiderlings release a deadly venom, which kills her.

Why Do They Do That?

The mom lets her spiderlings eat her because the nutrients will help them survive.

Giant Water Bugs

Water bug moms lay all the eggs. Then, they just sit back and take it easy. How do they get away with that?

WHAT?

The cunning moms glue their eggs on the water bug dad's back! So, he's literally stuck bringing up the kids!

MOM LETS DAD DO IT ALL!

Why Do They Do That?

Dad is just great at raising the babies.

Water bug moms choose dads that they think will be good parents. Moms prefer a mate who already has eggs on his back, because he has proved himself to be a caring dad.

Dad does push-ups underwater to keep water and air moving around the eggs. He bobs up to the surface now and then, too, to make sure the eggs have enough air.

The bug dad strokes the eggs with his back legs. This moves water over the eggs, keeping them clean. Once the eggs hatch, the young nymphs swim away, and dad's work is done.

Dung Beetles

Dung beetle babies are lucky compared to most insect babies. Mom and dad often both look after their offspring. The devoted parents prepare a lovely nursery for their babies—in poop!

WE RAISE THE KIDS IN A BALL OF POOP!

WHAT?

Dung beetles love moist poop. They suck out the smelly liquid inside. This dung soup is full of nutrients! Moms lay more eggs in the rainy season when the poop is squishy!

Dung beetles form some fresh poop into a ball. Then they roll it away.

Mom lays her eggs inside the ball. She seals it with dung, spit, and her own poop, and then buries it.

Sometimes mom helps push the dung ball. Or she hitches a ride as a lookout! Other dung beetles may try to steal it.

Why Do They Do That?

The larvae love a diet of dung! They eat the solid bits the adults don't like to eat. Burying animal dung helps loosen and feed the soil. It helps control flies, too, by taking away their food source.

Spiny Leaf Insects

This giant stick insect doesn't take much care when laying her eggs.

She uses her tail to fling the eggs onto the forest floor!

The eggs look like edible seeds. They are gathered by hungry ants and taken to their underground nest. Luckily, the ants just eat the outside of the eggs.

It doesn't matter if a bird eats a spiny leaf insect egg. They are covered in a coating that protects them. The bird just poops them back out again!

Stick insect moms don't need a dad to have babies! They can produce female babies without a mate.

WHAT?

When the eggs hatch, the nymphs look like baby ants. This doesn't fool the ants, but it does fool birds.

Birds don't like eating ants. The baby stick insects can escape into the trees without being eaten.

Why Do They Do That?

Adult stick insects are masters of disguise too. To keep from being eaten, they stay very still and look like a twig! Quickly flicking their eggs to the ground means they can stay in disguise.

The egg's coating cushions its fall and allows it to float in the water. The eggs attract ants, and pretending to be an ant then helps the nymphs survive. Smart!

Assassin Bug

With a name like "assassin bug," you know these guys are going to be trouble. No one is safe, not even their own children!

Why Do They Do That?

The dad assassin bug usually guards the eggs. He protects the eggs from parasitic wasps. Poor dad can't head off for a snack when he gets hungry. So, he starts to eat the eggs around the edges of the nest. He knows these are the most likely to get eaten by the wasps. And they are the most likely to have had wasp eggs laid inside them. See page 29 for the gruesome details!

tiny parasitic wasp

Some nymphs survive both dad and the wasps. They hatch by pushing up a plug that sealed the top of the egg. The nymphs often wear these comical plug hats until they **molt**!

As it grows, an insect must molt, or shed its old hard casing. A new, larger casing then hardens around them.

Assassin bugs stab their prey and inject a venom that starts to dissolve it. Then, they suck out their insides!

WHAT?

The assassin bugs' chief enemy is no charmer either. Parasitic wasps lay their eggs inside the eggs or bodies of other insects. Their larvae then eat their host!

Glossary

antennae Feelers on the head of a bug that help them sense their environment.

carcass The dead body of an animal, especially one that has been slaughtered for food or is rotting.

exoskeleton A hard, protective shell on the outside of some animals that acts as a skeleton.

larvae Insects after they hatch from an egg and before they change into their adult form.

nutrients Substances in food that help people, animals, and plants live and grow.

pupa A protective shell that a caterpillar forms while it transforms into a butterfly or moth.

trophic eggs Unfertilized eggs laid by some animals simply to provide food for their young.

venom A poisonous substance that some animals produce and inject into their prey or enemies through a bite or sting.

Index

antennae 4, 9
ants 4, 12, 13, 14, 15, 26, 27
assassin bug 28, 29

bees 4
beetles 4, 8, 9, 24, 25
black lace-weaver spiders 19, 20, 21
burying beetles 8, 9
butterflies, large blue 12, 13

caterpillars 5, 12, 13
chrysalis 5, 13
colonies 15

desert spiders 18, 19
dracula ants 14, 15
dragonflies 4
dung beetles 24, 25

eggs 5, 7, 8, 10, 12, 13, 15, 16, 17, 18, 20, 22, 23, 24, 25, 26, 27, 28, 29
exoskeleton 4

froghoppers 10, 11

giant water bug 22, 23

larvae 5, 9, 10, 11, 13, 14, 15, 16, 17, 25, 29
leaf miners 16, 17

nutrients 21
nymphs 27, 29

parasitic wasps 28, 29
praying mantis 6, 7
predators 11, 27
pupa 5, 13

queen ants 13, 15

spiderlings 18, 19, 20, 21
spiders 5, 18, 19
spiny leaf insects 26, 27

venom 5, 21, 29

webs 5
wings 4